Bone Dry

<u>Vol. II: The Chaos</u>

<u>Written by Kevin S. Scott</u>

Vol. II: The Chaos

ISBN: 9798394903731

Vol. II: The Chaos

This book is dedicated to anyone who has suffered, those still suffering, and those affected by mental health and/or addiction.

"all great change is preceded by chaos"

- Deepak Chopra

chaos

noun

cha·os 'kā-,äs

a

: a state of utter confusion

the blackout caused chaos throughout the city

b

: a confused mass or mixture

a chaos of television antennas

c

: a state of things in which chance is supreme

especially : the confused unorganized state of

primordial matter before the creation of distinct forms

d

: the inherent unpredictability in the behavior of a

complex natural system (such as the atmosphere, boiling water,

or the beating heart

so I showed you my habits
I called it "The Curse"
it was only the start
the downfall got worse
couldn't stop what I started
too late to reverse
so surprised that I made it
friends left in a hearse
mom watched my heart harden
while I slowly broke hers
I share with you my story
I'll start with this verse
I call this "The Chaos"
the part after "The Curse"
sharing each tragedy
each one even worse

the look in my eyes…
couldn't get myself straight
I made you uneasy
the person you hate
no bridge I won't burn
said I won't return
you're in or you're out
my offer was firm
I was on a warpath
no faith left in you
my family saw change
and I lost them all too
said "I won't turn my back"
something that you don't do
but I've been gone for so long
that I lost myself too

I seem angry to most
defenses set to attack
soul's bitter and cold
"better not turn your back"
this dark hole for a heart
leaves my blood running black
I only inherit the evil
the bad habits of Jack
never a concept of karma
my inner conscience is lack
with an insanity plea
"this guy is a quack"
so be cautious with conflicts
because I'm quick to attack
better not try to cross me
better not turn your back

it was the start of a family
first born, eighty eight
a brand new baby girl
mom and dad couldn't wait
we fought like most kids
didn't seem like the trait
but the older we grew
there was nothing but hate
and we share the same parents
the constant family debate
her angry little brother
now it's silence, our fate
'cause it runs in the family
we, one by one, separate
but that's just how we're built
we're born with family we hate

the name carried on
born in ninety one
number five was my father
number six was his son
pushed the limits too far
far beyond fun
then I woke up at thirty
thinking "what have I done?"
angry and alone
my temper had won
because once they knew me
I was back on the run
will there be number seven?
a daughter, a son
what if they chose my brother..
the decision undone

woke up in a daze
wiped the sleep from my eyes
my hands start to shake
find a drink, normalize
"what day is it now?…"
"was I out with the guys?…"
start the day with a struggle
now I swallow these lies
if I could only slow down
"can we please compromise…"
clean myself up again
go to work in disguise
I feel it approaching
my soul as it dies
went from pain in the morning
to funeral parlor cries

is death always silent
can you hear a sound
a thousand souls screaming
from six feet underground
no stories to share
no proof that I've found
but it seems dark and eerie
like no one's around
"and death doesn't scare me"
with bravery so profound
then it's quick with a tear
standing at the grave mound
so I ask myself this..
"does death have a sound?"
or do we perish in peace
resting quiet below ground

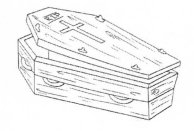

tormented by thoughts
guess you reap what you sow
and they keep coming back
like "The Raven" from Poe
and I'd love to escape
to be free and let go
but they're counting on smiles
so I put on a show
I ask "how are they happy?"
entering rooms with a glow
getting jealous of good times
wish my heart would just grow
but it feels like it's fate
"you could smile you know.."
if I could just free these demons
then the smiles could show

overwhelmed with it all
I feel quite out of place
as I tremble inside
"Lord, grant me some grace"
my anxiety climbs
they can tell by my face
and I'm usually friendly
but not in this case
I'd rather be all alone
with my thoughts, in the zone
I count my breaths til it's over
I count the time til I'm home

I cringe when they say it
your name is so painful
your secret I keep
that weekend in April
"can't happen to me"
now I've got the label
I was innocent then
but still I feel shameful
just a young naive boy
your actions, disgraceful
but still I stay silent
hide the family betrayal
ball my fists with your name
I can't help but be hateful
but you'll pay for your sins
and I'll strike when I'm able

I finally erupt
the look on their faces
they're getting too close
they don't know what space is
I pray for good news
the judge ruling court cases
I made a mistake
found myself in bad places
sharp dressed older men
hands clenching brief cases
he gives me a look
good news slowly changes
it's decided that day
they'll read my name on front pages

Vol. II: The Chaos

"let's go see the man"
the one that feeds my obsessions
he's not really a friend
we met through connections
he's got what I need
one of the devil's professions
not an honorable job
no retirement pensions
best keep your mouth shut
don't ask any questions
because he's quick to explode
he'll brandish his weapons
so let's make this one brief
before it's our lives he threatens

my memory had escaped me
popped a few on Woodthrush
I could feel myself changing
felt my face getting flush
saved a couple for morning
and the rest I would crush
washed it down with some whiskey
then my brain felt the rush

come home with aggression
sit with morbid reflection
have a drink for my sorrows
and a few pills I won't mention
let it all separate
the brain and body connection
as I float deeper now
gets hard to pay attention
am I awake or asleep
I'm in a different dimension
and just for a minute
I've lost all the tension
and just for a minute
I don't feel depression
until the sun comes again
and it's back to my profession

Vol. II: The Chaos

my brain is beside me, skin inside out, it
feels like a full moon, my lungs start to
shout, I fight with myself, another
murderous bout, blood runs from my eyeballs,
"he's crazy, no doubt," and the drugs start
to call, guess I can't go without, top it
off with some whiskey, licking drops from
the spout, a few hours to go, give some rain
to this drought, I could blame my genetics,
I could sit here and pout, I could wave the
white flag, I could finally tap out, but I
did it all, I decided this route, as I
mumble a prayer, through another blackout

now dripping with sweat
sprawled out on the floor
my prayers of survival
as I'm crushing one more
there's blood and there's vomit
on the seashell decor
my voice getting weak
I was just a sophomore
I'd cry out for help
even unlock the door
but it's now three AM
my voice lost in dad's snore
and I promised to stop
but tonight's a new war
so just let me see morning
let me make it to four

they used to break bones
but I never felt pain
I used to be a good guy
until I poisoned my brain
became a shell of a man
couldn't tell you my name
it was the opioid storm
I was caught in the rain
I called them my friends
but none of them came
they called me their brother
but we weren't the same
I watched it all burn
the spark and the flame
and that was the point
that's when I went insane

the man in the mirror
I hate who I see
the site of a stranger
I don't recognize me
my blood starts to boil
with my beastly view
as I say to myself
"I truly hate you"

take a good look
do you recognize me
the face of the devil
bringing you tragedy
do you remember me now
from your own robbery
I stole from you slow
captured your sanity
a thief in the night
brought your soul back with me
I swallowed you whole
made you my property

we made a home here
built brick by brick
but the walls start to crumble
the foundation won't stick
I could hear the bad news
the walls weren't very thick
my mind starts to race
now I make myself sick
I had to get out
had to leave this place quick
out the back door I ran
my exit was slick
and we may meet again
when I'm feeling homesick
but you won't see me coming
you'll just hear my gun click

we'd been here before
but you know how it goes
chasing a high
two weeks, the same clothes
never thought it would hit us
never thought overdose
too young for goodbyes
but these actions we chose
and we're fighting a war
that we're losing, it shows
my only hope for addiction..
is that the body count slows

always a race to the top
something to help me keep up
something stronger than coffee
no espresso in the cup
I twitch and sweat from the start
let the adrenaline build up
feel my heart start to race
begin my day at this pace
through the day in fast forward
with a ghostly look on my face
they can't see it's addiction
just a freak, a nutcase
but moving slow makes me think
and I hate the headspace
so I move a bit quicker
getting through the rat race

it's somewhat of a cycle
"at least it's not crack"
just so I can keep up
"better pick up the slack"
while some chill and vibe
I'm a head of the pack
going faster and faster
got this weight on my back
couldn't stop if I tried
I'll die from a heart attack
pull a pill from the drawer
a shock to my cardiac
and I call it a cycle
now an insomniac
sleepless nights from the speed
a fast paced maniac

if I could look deep inside
flip my eyeballs around
I can see myself thinking
hear a dull buzzing sound
find the root of the problem
why I'm so tightly wound
I'd confirm that I'm crazy
with the mess that I found

I once knew a guy
that no one called friend
a tale of young love
with the most tragic end
she hated his habits
dates and drugs never blend
she said to him one day
"I'm going out with a friend"
but you know what that means…
and heartache was a trend
so he dug himself deeper
hoping his wounds would mend
a new love in the liquor
now without a girlfriend
so he numbed himself more
and the romance was condemned

you were on top of the world, had the life
of your dreams, when you felt like a king,
or at least so it seemed, no one by their
side, no one heard their screams, you were
far out of reach, out plotting your schemes,
he now lays in a casket, and your brain
cannot grasp it, left to die all alone, the
only brother you've known, now you've got
your one wish, no more calls that you'll
miss, your family now broken, screaming "how
could he do this…" but we're the ones you
forgot, we're the ones you dismiss

I often freak out
I kill what is good
backed into a corner
the ground that I stood
I relive the past
times from my childhood
they tell me "just breathe"
but I would if I could
my words always twisted
often misunderstood
I don't get what I give
but I think that I should
if I could let down these walls
believe that I would
because I don't want to run
only be understood

we'll burn this place down
her words are the lighter
I keep myself quiet
the silent igniter
tensions get high
but I'm not a fighter
thinks my feelings are gone
I don't do it to spite her
the look on her face
fist clenching tighter
wasn't built for this war
I'm only a writer
it all starts to crumble
I can't put out this fire

I feel it approaching
my spirit's begun breaking
this knot in my stomach
my hands always shaking
and I let you down
heart constantly aching
and every day it's the same
another fight in the making
not allowed to feel sadness
blame the pills that I'm taking
you see me in hell
this mask, your mistaking
but I hurt when you hurt
and I break when you're breaking
if I could just fix it all..
the stress it's creating
if I could just feel your pain
stop your heart from this aching

when you're caught in the act
and you know right from wrong
you beg for forgiveness
the same old sad song
and you let people down
when you need to be strong
and your list of bad habits
grows incredibly long
you can't look at yourself
thinking "where'd I go wrong?"
but it's your funeral next
and they're playing your song

as I'm bit by the serpent
venom now in my veins
I reach for my wound
clothes soaked with blood stains
I fall to my knees
body riddled with pains
starts wrapping me tightly
now I'm locked in his chains
he takes his first bite
slowly eats my remains
the day that death chose me
as I wonder these plains

shook hands with the devil
I made him a deal
may sound like a joke
but the promise was real
I'd give up the smiles
for the pain that they feel
with Satan left in charge
now he took the wheel
could I fix it all..
their wounds would soon heal
I carried this burden
the pain was surreal
now I burn for their sins
my name in the newsreel

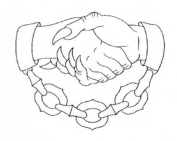

I see the fear on their face
I'm a villain, apparently
"you should probably get help"
"maybe seek out some therapy"
they all wince as I walk
every one of them scared of me
guess it's me against them
and I am the enemy
I was born with bad blood
so this must my destiny
but I'm ok being evil
"..you better tread carefully"
so don't test out my temper
you'll regret your choice terribly
because I'm the keeper of chaos
and sinister is my specialty

filled his mouth with such fury
but couldn't handle the taste
wasn't ready to hear it
this monster that he faced
found himself in hot water
rising up to his waist
couldn't stop what he started
heart pounding, it raced
between a rock and a wall
now he found himself placed
the mouse vs the monster
reputation disgraced
he bit too much to chew
wished this day was erased
now he hides in the corner
fearing the monster he faced

I was built for these sins
bad behavior came easily
swam in pools of bad blood
they would fear who I used to be
I was sharp as a knife
I cut them down so conveniently
put my anger on them
unleashed what's inside of me
I made fools of the brave
they'd regret how they doubted me
I would laugh as they crawl
cheering each vicious victory
but what I didn't know then
the thing that I couldn't see
this way of life, these sins
it was all slowly killing me

felt the guilt in your gut
your palms start to sweat
they're judging you now
heart's filled with regret
you feel like an outsider
and your actions upset
now they call you a monster
"you ain't seen nothin' yet"
wasn't that long ago..
how quick we forget
when we pushed them away
like we've never met

teenage years were a blur
can't account for most nights
filled our bodies with poison
brains were reaching new heights
some graffiti soaked walls
even ripped out the lights
young men with an ego
basement bare knuckle fights
and smoke filled every room
eyes red at the whites
a few of us lost control
watched as they read their rights
it's been a while since then
and I can't sleep most nights
went from punk kid to poet
the guy who just writes

it's becoming a pattern
"is this the fifth time?"
another one of them gone
another painful flatline
and they're dropping like flies
these close friends of mine
too young for a casket
they called this our prime
broken mothers and fathers
only left with a shrine
this deadly game that we play
just to have a good time

Vol. II: The Chaos

I could tell by the smell, we're approaching
the ocean, my summers spent as a kid, I
reminisce with emotion, my feet burned from
hot sand, my skin covered in lotion, we
would swim out too far, parents screamed in
commotion, we headed back to the house, we'd
shiver like we were frozen, then we stole
our dad's drinks, the flood gates were now
open, tender times as a kid, only to grow up
so broken, lost it all to the drink, that
devilish potion, had I only known then, this
future life to be chosen, I could have
avoided the pain, my demise, my implosion

Vol. II: The Chaos

they counted me out… spiritually torn in
half, soul lost in a wasteland, no chance of
a laugh, had conversations with a ghost, a
hell-sent holograph, locked away in the
nuthouse, I was feared by the staff, they
made me silent with scripts, spoke on my
behalf, and you can't trust the crazy, lies
through a polygraph, it was all gloom and
doom, this treacherous path, the decisions
that brought me, this dark aftermath, we'd
rebel in the mess hall, padded rooms,
psychopath, so it's one more for the
cuckoo's nest, drowning in the birdbath, so
keep these doors locked around me, beware of
my wrath, you'll never know my next move,
I'm a vicious psychopath

Vol. II: The Chaos

I sent out an S.O.S. but the sky with its
grays, my smoke out of site as my soul lay
ablaze, this new level of lonely, it'll
shock and amaze, no one by your side on your
darkest of days, I play it all back,
convince myself it's a phase, but it's
lodged in my brain, over and over it plays,
I tried their suggestions, "go out on
Fridays," and it worked for a bit, my mind
out of its maze, but I'm empty inside and
I'm stuck in my ways, so these smoke stacks
burn on as I watch the airways, so until
they come find me, I'll lay here and
stargaze

so I tried counting sheep
but the flock has me stressed
crazy thoughts in my head
and I feel like a guest
"you can sleep when you're dead"
but I'm just dying for rest
and it's all bottled up
need to get this off my chest
sleeping pills by the hundreds
"I think these will work best"
and I've tried every trick
even headed out west
now I ask God to help me
but this feels like a test
so how many more nights…
before my soul gets some rest

the pressure is constant
the weight begins crushing me
my bones start to break
this new sense of gravity
is it all in my head?
as I struggle with sanity
enemies eager now
they smile at my tragedy
no more letters home
goodbye to my family
another inch till I'm gone
I count my breaths anxiously
and then I wake from my sleep
another grim nightmare fantasy

another day on the road, another day that I
dread, as the sun hits my face, I crawl out
of this bed, I'll check for a text, go back
and read what she said, let her know that I
love her, wait 'til the message gets read,
counting the minutes to clock out, finally
go home and get fed "so how was your day?"
as we sit and break bread, stuff my face
till I'm fat, sleeping pills to the head,
say goodnight to my girl, then I see them
all dead, I'll go back and explain, you
probably think I'm insane, when I lay down
my head, and finally rest in my bed, my
dreams are so vicious, every one of them
dead, my family, my friends, I see only
bloodshed, I once murdered myself, saw me at
my deathbed, every dream feeling real, I
hang on by a thread, like they made me a
monster, and I only see red, like they made
me a villain, with the evil I spread, I
awake in such agony, "hey, it's all in your
head," then it's back on my feet, back to
days that I dread

remember that dream?
recall if you're able
the woman in my sleep
her features were fatal
but I can't look away
now locked in her cradle
the message was clear
the ending was painful
with her hair made of snakes
similar to the fable
turned me cold into stone
made me bitter and hateful

I drift off to sleep
every night is the same
I die in my sleep
I wake up in pain
nightmares every night
my subconscious to blame
we fight to the death
as they're cursing my name
a stab to the heart
or my skin set aflame
every night is a battle
and I'm losing this game
give me pleasant sleep
I don't mean to complain
put an end to these dreams
because I'm going insane

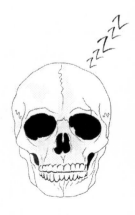

when you've tried counting sheep
but you're still wide awake
when you feel yourself tremble
and your hands start to shake
five, ten, maybe fifteen
how many pills does it take
and you force on a smile
but they know that it's fake
when they think that you're slipping
"relax for God's sake"
but the chaos is constant
and I just need a break
so I'm counting pills, counting sheep
every night still awake
maybe the sandman forgot me
maybe he made a mistake

it hurt when I heard it
now it's stuck in my head
it robs me of sleep
my skin crawls in this bed
I know I can't change it
and what's said has been said
but when I close my eyes
it's these thoughts that I dread
"you need to put it behind you"
say a prayer, look ahead
but it's my worst trait of all
I replay what they said

Dear Lord,

   Why does this feel like a test? It's a
struggle to sleep, and I can't seem to rest.
How much more can I take? Every night wide
awake. My mind full of madness, I think you
made a mistake. Why are the good days so
few? Torn between good and evil, seeking
guidance from you. When will the devil just
quit? This chip on my shoulder, feeling like
a misfit. I have so many questions, that I
thought you would know. Share with me your
strength, at my lowest of low. Like how you
stayed calm when they nailed you to the
cross. Now I'm losing sleep, and my mind's
at a loss. So I'm praying to you to help me
again, show my conscience some calmness..

        I need you,

            Amen

when it feels like my last breath
when my dreams feel like death
body soaking with sweat
repeat the words I regret
erupting with anger
they take my tone as a threat
when I sound like a villain
my loved ones always upset
they're scared of me now
they flinch at my silhouette
they tremble with fear
the worst that they've ever met
I'm a spawn of the devil
gave my soul for a debt
I'm the one that you run from
I'm the worst that you've ever met

everything's out of reach
my heartbeat has an echo
I hear a voice in the room
see a face in the shadow
I reach for relief
breathe the taste of tobacco
count my breaths, in and out
try to slow down the tempo
my nightmares wide awake
this anxious feeling that I know
as I pray to the sandman
as I talk to the shadow

hang up my horns for the night
make my way up the stairs
rest my bones in the bedroom
try to practice these prayers
"you made me a monster!"
one of your deadliest heirs
I can show you, I'm gentle
not that anyone dares
with the smirk of a serpent
people fall from their chairs
I send chills down your spine
I can stand up your hairs
I pray to God for some change
but I don't think that he cares
I can feel their eyes on me
I can feel all their stares

I wrote it all out
I told you my dreams
vivid visions of death
couldn't silence their screams
got some peace for a while
but it's back, so it seems
so I struggle to sleep
even tried counting sheep
and when I do drift away
when I've gotten too deep
past horrors return
my demons will creep
until I hear a faint ringing
my alarm starts to beep
off to work once again
trying to just earn my keep

when the earth changes shape
when your world starts to spin
you begin seeing double
and everyone has a twin
when you've lost your perception
got goosebumps on the skin
it's just the start of the day
let the nausea begin
and every step is a struggle
every wall, paper thin
a couple hours from home
vertigo setting in
I've lost my mind once before
but this is the worst that it's been
hallucinations now sober
insomnia is my sin

Vol. II: The Chaos

it's been a long time
haven't talked for a bit
I gave up reaching out
no replies, so I'll quit
to say that I miss you
something I wouldn't admit
the way you light up a room
your hilarious wit
and I hate how it ended
the way our family just split
when I couldn't see you
parents wouldn't permit
but I'd still love to talk
we can chat for a bit
so I'm here when you're ready
maybe think about it

will you finally miss me
when I'm brought home in a bag
but there's no fancy service
no pristine folded flag
and you're deep in your thoughts
smoking to the last drag
precious times as a kid
two boys playing tag
you were my only friend
"I'm with him," as I'd brag
but it's been a long time
"are you there?.." as I'd nag
like we've lost all those years
"oh yeah, him.." as you gag
and I'll be crying your name
when I wave the white flag

"so how are you doing?"
I shrug with, "I'm fine"
the look on my face
now they see the sign
a rough couple days
and I don't want to whine
no desire to write
can't make the words rhyme
"so what makes you happy?"
"no idea, no time"
and that man in the mirror
sends chills down my spine
so I say what they want
change the subject, decline
let them tell me their secrets
while I refuse to share mine

I know they all say it
didn't want to believe it
that all those good things
they come to an end
I feel like a kid
like I lost a true friend
was it just me
the kind of message I send
was it too much
the emotions I penned
I should not be surprised
this outcome's a trend
but I thought just for once
this good thing wouldn't end

When you put your happiness in
the hands of others, you
must make a friend of
misfortune.

who would go first, we'd sit and we'd stew,
   felt a lump in my throat, with the short
straw that I drew, this outcome was painful,
what was I to do, my fist pounded the table,
   my face a shade blue, was it my death or
theirs, a thought I would chew, I fight with
myself, this war I go through, a rage builds
 inside, this anger that grew, was this life
for me, this karma I'm due, I turn to these
fellows, the rough rugged crew, as I whisper
      "I'm out," and I quickly withdrew

you think they don't notice
when you're falling apart
when you've lost the connection
from your head to your heart
you think you can hide it
like your tactics are smart
but you've gotten too deep
and you can't stop what you start
the master of emotions
you even think it's an art
with few feelings left
those too will depart
they all watch it happen
some even take part
until you're lost all together
and it's too late to restart

your pulse in your ears
you can hear a pin drop
the mind starts to wander
and time comes to a stop
you feel yourself start to lose it
you're going crazy up top
the sound of your heartbeat
sets the tone, the backdrop
conversations with me
I sit back and eavesdrop
voices raised to a roar
eye sheds a teardrop
their outbursts rage on
puts me over the top
I need to silence the voices
because they're talking nonstop

I've been breaking up fights
been playing referee
constantly caught in the middle
must be my destiny
"keep it clean boys"
preparing their weaponry
I dance in the ring
I chose my steps carefully
bloody battles before me
it weighs on me heavily
I announce him the victor
I raise his hand dreadfully
another murderous bout
this weight crushes me
always caught in the middle
another late night it'll be

Vol. II: The Chaos

I'm cold to the bone
won't find a heartbeat
they once called me a con man
but it's now death I can't cheat
I reflect on mistakes
bad times on the street
but it's all catching up
and this end's bittersweet
with my final day closing in
as I feel this defeat
let these tales be a lesson
let these sins not repeat

when the tears start to dry
emotions quite raw
and your heart starts to melt
when the ice starts to thaw
you've got stories of horror
tales of shock and awe
and you swore you would quit
"this is the last straw"
you're stuck in this hell
you climb and you claw
and the evil you've seen
"the worst that I ever saw"
so it's time that you run
when you finally withdraw
because good times never last
when you pull the short straw

when our egos come first
when we don't want to talk
do we speak out of anger?
think it through as we walk?
our worst weapon of all
usually comes as a shock
when we're sharp with our tongue
when we insult and mock
it gets the best of us all
some delete numbers and block
but with anger and me
that's not a door I can lock
so we face it head on
apologize, have a talk
because when my door's closed too long
I know the devil will knock

so the chaos caught up
let the cleansing begin
time to pay for my actions
release the demons within
strapped to tables and chairs
Thorazine pierced the skin
controlled the chaos within me
saliva ran down my chin
"everyone now repent!"
my head starts to spin
heard screams through the night
these walls are so thin
"we're just here to help you"
said the wolf in sheepskin
"how did I get here?"
locked in the looney bin
they were breaking my spirit
destroying me from within

couldn't stand by my word
they nailed me to the cross
broke the news to my mother
"I'm sorry for your loss"
next the storm and the flood
the water turned to blood
lightning struck at nightfall
and the storm cleansed us all
our sins washed away..
my soul in free-fall
a nightmare of a day
if I do recall
but now free of this evil
my skin doesn't crawl
the water washed away
and my death, a close call

no stranger to chaos
I'm good with destruction
you've read it before
the heartache I mention
with fists clenching tight
this room fills with tension
but they've had enough
a hard intervention
the problem was me
I knew the first session
I laid it all out
a painful confession
my soul felt a change
I lost the aggression
I was free of this curse
and I lost the obsession

used to idolize evil
my hero was a mobster
I turned to bad habits
I turned to a monster
controlled by the money
a soldier on the roster
but I was poisoned inside
and mom cried to the doctor
I needed a change
they'd rescue this martyr
couldn't relate to the books
until I found the right author
and with this new change
my acceptance was broader
I was saved from my sins
and I'll live a bit longer

Vol. II: The Chaos

at what point did you realize
our souls are all black
there's no hope for the babies
they're all hooked on crack
we can't trust each other
afraid to turn our back
used to count happy days
but I think we lost track
we numb our emotions
poisons pulled off the rack
a glass of wine for the girls
while the boys drown in jack
is this your way of life?
is your mind out of whack
come with me on this ride..
we'll get your happiness back

those dreams were a warning
faces of people I knew
they told me to stop
saw a deadly preview
heading straight for the grave
finally had a breakthrough
sought the help of a doctor
said the warning was true
looking back on my habits
now my life in review
to pay a debt for my sins
and now the payment is due
but with a chance to restart
to give this life a re-do
I share with you my story
I'll be here to warn you

didn't like who I was
I was carefree on a spree
put the blame on the booze
but the problem was me
I would drink till I'm dead
couldn't break myself free
"you won't last too long"
my doctors death guarantee
it helps to numb when we hurt
I know you'd probably agree
but every morning it's back
another black out by three
for the vicious cycle to stop
I had to change me
the alcohol was a symptom
and I wasn't able to see
I always numbed what was broken
ignored the pain to a degree
and it took years to be happy
something I couldn't foresee
but once I could see the problem
without the booze referee
I learned who I was
and that the problem was me

I couldn't slow down
I just needed more
my habits turned evil
fighting a mental war
even lied to my family..
"I'm clean" and I swore
couldn't show them the truth
hid my stash in a drawer
my head and my heart
a constant tug-a-war
I held on by a thread
passing out on the floor
but I couldn't keep up
this life was a chore
then I waved the white flag
I couldn't fight anymore

when you turned to a monster, a nightmare
come true, it was your life or mine, it was
me versus you, and so I struck first, my
dagger piercing straight through, watch the
blood pool around us, your face turning
blue, thought of myself as a hero,
preventing the damage you'll do, and so I
left the blood trail, leading straight back
to you, they found your body still warm,
moist with fresh morning dew, I stayed away
from the windows, a recluse, I withdrew, and
so life carried on, a fresh start, I'm brand
new, but I still say to the mirror, "we
killed the old you"

"maybe I'll just relocate"
a new life in transit
a new chance to restart
leave this town for a bit
blamed my problems on places
waved goodbye as I split
I was overwhelmed with unknown
taken back, I admit
unpacked my demons and settled
"I really hope I make it"
a thousand miles behind me
and after a week it had hit
I travel like a tornado
never stop, destroy it
and every place is the same
I never quite seem to fit
so when you're running from trouble..
stop and think about it
your problem's not with the places
but what your place is in it

your palms start to sweat
your pulse in your ears
the room's turning cold
as you face all your fears
their eyes are like daggers
this view of your peers
now you let it all go
what's inside all those years
and the room full of strangers
one by one, disappears

when your mind is a mess
and you're feeling the stress
when you can't leave your bed
and you're feeling hopeless
and they all start to worry
"I've been better I guess"
and they want you to visit
but it's hard to say yes
when you fight with yourself
a mind game of chess
now you need to get up
let's build your success
and when those thoughts come again
try not to obsess
just take a deep breath
and try your best not to stress

steam rose from the ground
the cold morning air
the sun creeps in the distance
the view has this glare
I move slow in the morning
make my way to the chair
gaze off in the distance
enjoy this view as I stare
I reflect on the past
when I lived without care
bones now old and brittle
I live more aware
the past and the present
hard to even compare
on cold autumn mornings
with this beauty out there

one deep breath
and I let it go
my soul vibrates
with the stereo
bad days now gone
from the audio
there's peace in my pulse
and I'm breathing slow
the cool autumn air
the taste of Marlboro
the day that it hit me
the day that I let it go

unplug my brain for the night
cruise along to the melody
I try to tune out the noise
find a moment of clarity
the constant chaos of life
when finding peace is a penalty
the roaring volume of voices
I ignore what they're telling me
and it's all dog-eat-dog
I'm the only one helping me
it's the rich and the poor
I don't buy what they're selling me
so at this time of day, this ride
it's pure ecstasy
my only chance to escape
the way I soothe myself mentally

I dreamt of a world unseen
I was young and adventurous
a place where the sun never set
and the laughs were so effortless
and there were never bad days
I felt a love with such tenderness
what a thought as a kid
a world that was generous
but the older I grew
the less I was curious
and I've aged colder now
because this world is so dangerous
and that dream as a kid
it now seems so humorous
because our happiness now
only comes from our purchases

let's just talk it out
no heated debate
tell me your troubles
give me an update
I'm here to just listen
release all your hate
put the burden on me
release all this weight
so start from the top..
I'll sit here and wait
say it all or a little
I'll let you elaborate
because I know that I hurt you
and this apology came late

am I seeing it now
are my eyes finally open
it was always just noise
but now I hear what is spoken
and it hurts a bit now
thinking that we're all broken
all those years as a kid
back when time was just frozen
but I'm much older now
maybe a little outspoken
and it's painful to watch
like my future's been stolen
if I could just fix them all
no one by their lonesome
and if that's all it took
a few words and a poem

I could share stories of sadness
and situations quite scary
wasn't always blue skies
no little house on the prairie
a couple brushes with death
situations quite hairy
rather shocked I'm alive
nights praying "Hail Mary"
mixed poisons repeatedly
my selections would vary
these stories would shock you
when life used to be scary
but at the time of it all
the chance of death didn't scare me
still shocked I'm alive
guess God thought he would spare me

I dig up the demons
pull back the disguise
I rip up the pages
the tempers will rise
the times I was selfish
when I told them lies
it's all such a blur
the daze in my eyes
leave it all here
the resentment that dies
reflecting on me
and the wreckage of highs
let it all go
now say your goodbyes
and set your soul free
from the ones you despise

body's on autopilot
I've got nothing upstairs
consciousness cancels out
mental musical chairs
and it's another sad story
can't relate to their shares
and who has it worse…
now we're just splitting hairs
I'd share my own curse
not that anyone cares
with him hurting back home
feeling the burden he bears
he keeps to himself
nursing his new repairs
with a story that's written
on the scars that he wears

fluorescent lights flicker
moans and groans of the weary
the place we all dread
tone of the room, dark and eerie
it rips you to shreds
someone you love dearly
we assume it's the worst
anxiety high with our theory
and it happened so fast
from smiles to dreary
when we feel bulletproof
then we get hurt severely
with your family all there
to have someone with me
it feels good to be chosen
with the people that picked me

the anxiety climbs
as I stepped out of this shell
the room is quite eerie
a faint chemical smell
and I know they're concerned
"I hope it goes well"
but this place is bad news
my own version of hell
and it's shown on my face
they think I'm unwell
as they ask me some background
some secrets to tell
they tell me relax
overhead plays Adele
there's a doctor with bad news
broken parents now yell
the room's flooded with sadness
teary eyes start to swell
"no news is good news"
then I bid them farewell
feeling sad for the sick
"goodbye sir, be well"

Vol. II: The Chaos

when I couldn't hang on, when my faith
wasn't strong, wasn't much of a believer,
occasionally comfort a griever, but I had
these mental scars, years lost at the bars,
I was out of my mind, I was too drunk to
drive cars, but when I drank I fit in.. the
old men smoked cigars, when no one was a
stranger, and good times would be ours,
they'd all gather round, we played our
guitars, but I still hated me.. my mind
locked behind bars, I'd pour my heart out..
these songs were memoirs, and my idea of
God.. was a man in the stars, but one day it
hit me.. it took four padded walls, it took
them to commit me, wasn't a punishing God,
my sins wouldn't kill me, all alone in the
darkness, I felt someone with me, it was my
second chance and death nearly gripped me,
so I changed my behavior, now I don't live
so risky, and I can still have a good time
but I don't need the whiskey, so with a
chance and a prayer I might live to see
fifty

we try to do right
but this sin stained my soul
a storm of bad karma
as I crawl out of this hole
I could point a finger
but I played a role
the lives that I hurt
the youth that I stole
it weighs on me heavy
storm clouds take a toll
but just as I'm breaking
as I might lose control
I come back to earth
take a breath, take a stroll
because the past is behind me
and happiness is the goal

I'm sorry for the rage
the bad times that you witness
always fighting a war
my mind with this sickness
am I Jekyll or Hyde
the arguments during Christmas
when I tore it apart
when I don't mind my business
you just don't understand
it's my brain, it's this illness
and how quickly I turn
from vulnerable then to viscous
it explains why I hide
in my thoughts with a stillness
try to find the right answer
maybe ask for forgiveness

a wolf in by sheep's clothing..
I can say that I knew some
memories in my sleep
my nightmares were gruesome
used to dance with the devil
mixed poisons, abused 'em
then out came the wolves
and boy did I feel dumb
I pray for them now
and hope good days do come
because this past used to haunt me
but I've managed some freedom

to say when we're wrong
ain't natural for most
to be vulnerable
leave our sins all exposed
we're quick with good news
"look at me" as we boast
but when we've screwed up
we keep our mouth closed
and it doesn't phase some
no regret, not opposed
but for people like me
this burden's a ghost
so I'm sorry to you
for the harm I imposed
now I start the next chapter
say goodbye to this ghost

everyday's a fresh start
another chance that we get
do we wake up with anger
do we finally forget
they're watching you closely
as they lay down their bet
entertained by your madness
like it's Russian roulette
show them a new side
let those wagers sweat
because when they've lost control
you become a new threat

always drowned my emotions
to stop was to die
mixed the drugs and the booze
couldn't bare being dry
those dark inner feelings
brings a tear to your eye
so your numbing yourself
I was that type of guy
but I saw my life flash before me
it even seemed like goodbye
so I took my demons head on
gave this life a retry
and it took time to find peace
"I'm ok" with a sigh
but now I float a bit different
with this happiness high

Vol. II: The Chaos

let this be a voice, for the lives
devastated, a special place in the text, the
lost souls dedicated, they don't know
there's relief, addiction's uneducated, try
to do it ourselves, drugs and drinks
medicated, so scared to speak up, "help
me.." hesitated, they saw us as losers, we
got high, levitated, and that used to be
me.. then their words resonated, felt a new
kind of high, mentally elevated, spoke of
hero's and hope, their words marinated, so
if you feel like you're lost, I can say I
related, I can show you a change, you and I,
now acquainted, this gift of new life, for
the old one that I traded

wasn't big on believing, never prayed to the
Lord, church Sunday's with mom, the sermon
had me bored, led a life full of sin, live
and die by the sword, and my habits were
filthy, warning signs I ignored, I'd reach
bottom again, then my faith was restored, I
needed a change, so this faith I explored, I
would speak to strong men, threw my sins
overboard, then I felt this new feeling, I
was shocked, I was floored, and I never
turned back, a new life, my reward, and I
speak to him daily, my new friend in the
Lord

let me tell you a story, a tale about liars,
he was different than most, had a couple
loose wires, walked with clouds over head,
they all knew of his priors, but to only fit
in.. one of his deepest desires, found
happiness for a bit, this new crew of
insiders, but the good times were short-
lived, the happiness that expires, and the
rage slowly grew, his soul burning with
fires, all the pain ate at him, struck him
deep in his fibers, he had a very short
fuse, walked the world wearing blinders, "I
think the problem is me.." - "what's the
work it requires?" wouldn't be a quick fix,
adjust his gears with some pliers, what he
didn't know then, he'd soon work with
advisors, he'll have to lay it all out, with
the shrink he soon hires, he'll tell them
his story, share his deepest desires, and
it'll be hard at first, tell them about all
his priors, help him find some new friends,
maybe other outsiders, "this work lasts a
lifetime" the journey that never expires,
"were not trying to change you.." - "just
reroute your wires"

Vol. II: The Chaos

Vol. II: The Chaos

Mental Health Crisis Lines / Suicide Hotlines

Suicide and Crisis Lifeline –
Dial - 988

Trevor HelpLine /Suicide Prevention
for LGBT+ Teens 1-866-488-7386

Crisis Text Line- Text HOME to
741741

Gay & Lesbian National Hotline
(1-888-843-4564)

National Runaway Safeline-
1-800-RUNAWAY (chat
available on website)

Teenline
310-855-4673 or
Text TEEN to 839863
(teens helping teens)

Drug and Alcohol

National Council on Alcoholism and
Drug Dependence (NCADD)
1-800-622-2255

Partnership for Drug-Free Kids
1-855-DRUGFREE
or text your message to 55753

Substance Abuse and Mental Health
Services Administration (SAMHSA)
1-800-662-4357

Alcoholics Anonymous:
aa.org

Narcotics Anonymous:
na.org

Heroin Anonymous:
heroinanonymous.org

Friends and Family of Alcoholics
al-anon.org

Friends and Family of Addicts
nar-anon.org

Vol. II: The Chaos

Violence and Abuse

National Domestic Abuse Helpline
1-800-799-7233
Text "Start" to 88788

Gang Violence – Victim Support Services
425-252-6081

National Sexual Assault Hotline
800-656-4673

National Helpline for Male Survivors
1in6.org

National Street Harassment Hotline
855-897-5910

National Center for Victims of Crimes
855-4-VICTIM (84-2846)

National Human Trafficking Hotline
888-373-7888

National Center for Missing and Exploited
Children
800-843-5678

For questions or comments on the book:
bonedrypoetry@gmail.com

For poetry posted daily find me on
Instagram: @bone.dry.poetry

Editing by Lauren Bukenas & Amanda Leone

Illustrations by Lou Hansen

Photography by Kevin Seger